A Sure Connection

"At times a love letter to the natural world, at others a poignant reminder of love, loss and hope, Herring's poems are a sensitive probe of the small moments that create our most lasting memories. Strung together like little jewels, the many facets of each memory reflect back to us our complicated connection with the world around us. Occasional glimpses of a wider world and a sprinkle of literary references add depth to one woman's search for *A Sure Connection*."

~ Penny Draper, Author/Columnist

A Sure Connection

Poems

W.M. Herring

NON CANADA

Publisher's note: This book is a work of fiction. Names, characters, places and incidents are either the product of the author's imagination or are used fictitiously, and any resemblance to actual persons living or dead is entirely coincidental.

Lifeline, written by W.M. Herring, © *The Christian Century*, appears by permission.

Library and Archives Canada Cataloguing in Publication

Title: A sure connection : poems / W.M. Herring.

Names: Herring, W. M., author.

Description: Poems.

Identifiers: Canadiana 2021025758X | ISBN 9781989689288 (softcover)

Classification: LCC PS8615.E76875 S87 2021 | DDC C811/.6—dc23

Printed and bound in Canada on 100% recycled paper.

Now Or Never Publishing
901, 163 Street
Surrey, British Columbia
Canada V4A 9T8

NONPUBLISHING.COM
Fighting Words.

We gratefully acknowledge the support of the Canada Council for the Arts
and the British Columbia Arts Council for our publishing program.

Dedicated to my children, to their children,
and to the generations who will follow all of us.

Contents

Three Black Dogs

We agree to take two dogs.
Any kind, even ill ones—I will play the vet.
Just for Christmas, to give them a break,
to fill the dull moments in an adult household.
Yes. Just for Christmas.

She paces behind a barrier
in this barking shelter,
breaking stride to cough.
Skin and bones and nerves.
        Who is more afraid?
Oh, the strong black head, deep eyes—
        she will be a handsome dog.

Here, now, is the other—
twelve days old,
a mere handful of possibility.

We cannot leave them: we take the dogs.

When did our first black dog appear?
        A ghost dog, a vapour seeping in.
Such a quiet infiltration, hardly sensed.
        His gnawing stills all appetite;
        his growls punctuate the night,
        destroy all hope of sleep.

The pup grows so quickly.
Napping in my husband's lap
her legs stretch beyond his knees.
        They twitch and bend, searching for support.
On good days the black beast naps, too.
At last, so does the man.

In the tall late-summer grass I rise high
above the dogs in sight and foresight.
They search the ground, captive to their
senses, alert to sign of mouse or deer.
They do not spy the buck at meadow's edge
straighten and slip into the woods.

Priding myself on disaster prevented
I pull toys from my sack.
        Two dogs as one
        look up, wag tail,
        ready for the game.
But scents drift by and the dogs run off.
I whistle and wait.

The Rule:
Wait fifteen minutes, go home,
make a cup of tea, sit at the window,
wait some more. They will return.

This primal black dog is heavy.
He leans on your chest and you cannot breathe.
When he exhales you cannot think.
But, some days, some days, prayer
is answered and he forgets to come.

The Rule:
If you have a cup of tea, wait fifteen minutes
and he doesn't come, it is a fine day.

Surely, this dread dog will soon wane.
He may sleep in a forgotten corner.
He will lose his way.

One morning we will look and listen.
We will count them once, twice and again:
there will only be two dogs.

Ever-After Birds

The week my brother took to his bed
I took to knitting in the leather chair—
formed small birds of smooth
cotton yarn when I wasn't
        scrubbing and bleaching
        washing and folding
        praying and weeping
        striding in the rain.

The creatures fell from my needles
        another upon the others
unadorned, plain and simple.

Life Birds, Death Birds, Ever-After Birds:
a flock of doves to number the days.

Easy Grace

A fine morning in the ninth month
migrant birds lately flown
round rosehips grown glossy red
uncut hay well lodged,
wet from last night's rain—
cirrostratus cloud strafes scattered
rays across thunder-struck sky.

Boreal chickadee lands
on a willow branch
feels it sway under the burden,
fluffs feathers to catch
some tender warmth
rising since sunrise,
accepts provision of the day
seems not to yearn
for some other plan.

My fond hope:
to find a place
and settle in
with such easy grace.

Winter Lexicon

Freeze-Up

If you are the type to bury a horse,
not drag it out back for the coyotes,
cast a discerning eye on that
aged gelding before freeze-up.
If he moves stiff-legged and bunchy
in autumn's pasture, he'll surely
get worse. Summon the vet
and the backhoe,
coax him into the sun
for a feed of sweet grain.

Black ice

Sun flirts with hills through the Cariboo.
Late afternoon glazes shade with black ice.
The truck ahead slides over the line.
Quick! Douse the engine fire!
Talk to the guy, hold his bleeding neck.
It is OK; the ambulance is coming.
You are safe. It is OK, OK.

I plunge my bloodied
clothes in the washtub
troubled by one thought—
what was his name?

Last Snow

We thought the last snow fell a week ago
did not believe that it could snow again.
Reclassify last week's event—penultimate.

Lynx Canadensis

Evenings I become expert on the Lynx
—study conformation and habit, habitat and range.
By day I comb forest trails for a sign,
a glimpse of the cat I know is there.
Mid-March I happen on two kill sites—
        grainy carmine halos on white crust
        close by prints of great padded paws.

Thaw

Roof-drips in the night
announce this thaw
        with gentle wind
        with spruce branch swirls,
        tips held by phantom hands.
On the track, season shift
grabs me by one boot
sunk deep in rotten snow.

Rotten ice

Below the stacked-log dam
ice rots along a channel
worn by seepage and otter holes.
The farmer listens from her log house:
snow machines race along the ridge
jump the berm, whack the ice.
She awaits the shouts or swift
and sudden silence.

Swimmers

1.
A prairie university celebrates
the new pool by mandating
swimming classes, eight lengths required.
He learns the side stroke, his only stroke.
Quick, take a picture!
1935, Geology and Chemistry:
smiling face, convocation gown,
wet trunks against his skin.

2.
A girl in flowered swimsuit
snug rubber bathing cap,
of slender build, composed,
stands determined at pool's edge
arms raised for the perfect entry.
Caption in the Gazette reads:
Rosemount Hopeful Takes Meet, 1935
means working class girl, the one
who learned to swim in a lake,
brother coaching after he scrutinized
practices at the country club when he
should have been tending the lawn.

3.
My father is already in the water
when I leave the #2 bus at Kits Beach—
shallow ripples, shoulder and head,
thin brown hair dry, perfectly combed.
His satisfied grin widens when
he perceives me across the lawn.

He glides back and forth
aside the seawall of the pool
thirty minutes by the clock.
I catch him on film,
make patient daisy chains
eager for the bus ride together,
anticipating dinner.

4.
Northern lakes are cool, so my mother
does not swim on camping trips.
Once, late afternoon
at the Cave and Basin pool,
she removes her beach coat
slips into the water,
effortlessly, flawlessly,
executes the Australian crawl
until they close, tell us to leave.
There is no photo, only
the image in my mind—
sharper than Kodachrome.

Gleann Eilg: Lennon's Tuba

"I'm an artist and if you give me a tuba,
I'll bring you something out of it."
John Lennon

Give me a tuba,
a thousand silent tubas:
shining caps upon the waves
broad bells skyward
bouncing bright
before the storm
sinking in the basin
flashy as silvered fish.

Give me a tuba,
a dozen off-pitch tubas:
lumpish and discoloured
a raucous band of geese
rolling down the turf
dissonant canon of
barks and honks.

Give me a tuba,
a solitary tuba:
a burnished grey seal
elegant and sleek
set upon gabbro shelf
uttering long lament.
He entreats Orca to depart,
serenity to return.

Night Passage

Drawn by skiff of fresh snow
I trek at dawn to the field seeking
crisp prints with tales of night passage.

Coyote travels alone, exits the woods
by the beaver dam, lopes between saplings
at field's end, toward the main trail.
She does not wander nor change her gait.
Is she here to celebrate the moon?

Two deer leave the main trail and cross that field
headed for open water—the runoff stream
below the dam. They need a cool drink
before they rest. There is no haste.

The hare carries on beside the deer track then stops.
No movement forward, no retreat.
This story is penned in wingtip-ruffled snow.
An odyssey ends and an owl glides away.

Little Junco

A flock of birds has taken
to the bird-berry bush by the lane—
six or seven dark-eyed juncos
bird-busy in the mist.
They flit in and out, up and down,
perform an odd scratching dance
hop ahead hop back
with claws a-drag
separating seed from gravel
fussing in the dirt.

These passerines grace
the monochrome morning
with their desert palette plumes
        sooty black of boulder
        rosy blush of sand
        drab brown of lizard
        ivory of high-valley cloud
save for one albino
who shares their manoeuvres
artlessly or mimics well.

She moves among them as
some alabaster holy bird,
or nothing more than
another smells-right
acts-right little junco.

WHAT THE LITTLE PORTUGUESE FORGOT

"Sonnet 43, Sonnets from the Portuguese"
Elizabeth Barrett Browning

With a sure hand the crust is easy:
poke with a fork
load it with marbles
bake until done.

The lemon layer:
... the mixture is thick and translucent
... continue to cook, stirring, at least
three more minutes—the mixture
will plop off the spoon in clumps.
As the morph from thick fluid to clump
exceeds three minutes, then five and ten
discount Fanny's advice,
keep stirring as you fall
into memories of lemon—
tart patisserie flan
sorbet treats at dusk
scented avenues.

Sculpt meringue in perfect peaks
stand guard as top heat blankets
each pinnacle in gold.

After dinner, show her what
the little Portuguese forgot:
lemon meringue pie.

Last Feed

No one wants to draw
last feed in winter
don layers of mismatched clothes
and trudge into the dark.
Sometimes two will go
for company, or to catch up.

Inside the paddock our cold and
stumbling trek takes reward
in sweet breath from the beasts.
We fill bins, muck stalls, spread hay.

As we turn for home,
a sudden shade falls
between us and the moon:
a winged form sweeps by
        broad and low.

Gleann Eilg: The Outhouse

He has a notion
        somewhat less
        than half a mind
to pull down the
sorry rhombohedron
that blocks the eastward view
from cottage kitchen to
sloped and saturated turf
where half-grown geese
land and browse, to suss out
no doubt, long-term lodgings.

Since he has no proper sightline
those birds are well stuck in
before he releases the mutts,
attempts to instill the Fear of Dog.

He will tear down the privy
preserve rusty implements
        years ago hung on sawn planks
        wrest them now from rot and moss
study exposed terrain in morning sun
learn to cut the geese some slack.

The Red Journal

The red journal lives
on the all-sorts table
by the best-view window:
repository for fragments
one per scribbled line.

This week she adds:
snake closet
wood smoke
it is enough
palmar crease.

Here is fertile ground,
sower and seed.
Pray for sunshine,
count on rain.

Late November, -10C

I forgot to tell you, to say,
        (that time you went for so long
        came back somewhat changed)
forgot to say:

The barred owl was there
in the paddock at four o'clock
on a stump, hunting mice
catching distilled, chilled amber air.
He lifted off, banked aside the barn,
settled in an aspen by the fence.
Crows massed from nowhere,
everywhere, scolded, circled
as though something
was dead or should be.

The owl slid off the branch
        almost liquid
slipped under the bare willow
the swaying heads of grass.
The crows flew east, shed
gloaming from their tails.

I rushed up the hill, up home:
I thought you might be there.

Thresholds

When toddler and grandmother
follow the garden path
ready to pick peas
they happen upon a steaming
pile of bear scat.
They calmly turn back
to the house without the peas.
Taking fifty dollars from her
purse, laying it on the table
the woman simply says
        Buy the boy a dog.

Soon we have a free-to-good-country-home
dog and another outdoor rule:
When the dog barks, go inside.
No questions asked, no debating the cause—
        squirrel or grouse, bear or
        Henry's bull out for a wander
        because Henry's on a bender
        and doesn't know he's strayed.

The rule holds—dog and children play their parts.

But when the dog barks by
the road, won't break off at
my whistle, I dismiss the rule.
I warily leave the yard to see what's up.
From road's edge I hear high pitched
chatter of a sow treeing her cubs.

In an instant she crosses the ditch
completes her bluff, huffing
and balanced on hind legs.

With no thought for the dog
I retreat a few paces then
hightail it for home.
The dog slips by as I
cross the threshold.

At Ten to Eight

I picture my mother in her tidy house
wearing pink pajamas and beaded hairnet.
She walks around checking things
        door locks
        window latches
        orderly rows of shoes
counting things
        newspapers in a pile
        streetlights that stretch from
        her house to the main road.
If lamps have burned out, she alerts the police.

She is alone—her companion left at seven.
At eight she will watch TV, go to bed.
I call at ten to eight.

Hi Mom
Hi. You got me here. I'm fine.
I'm glad. Did you have a nice day?
I'm fine.
Do you have your pills?
They are all closed.
Can you open the one that says Tuesday?
OK.
Can you take the pills in it?
OK.
Are you ready for bed?
I'm going to catch my show.
Yes. Then it will be time for bed.

Oh! I need something.
I need a piece of thin
cotton for my nose.
Do you need a tissue?
OK.
It's time for your show.
I'll call tomorrow.
Please come again.
I'll call tomorrow. Love you.

Memories on Deck

1. Narrow sun-faded boards
        spaced to let the rain
        down and frustrate rot
    detain the toddler in the house.
    He stares out the doorway
    through those gaps to the sloped
    ground below. His vertigo grants
    the morning breeze free entry.

2. A hummingbird held
    captive between two
    boards, feet in the crack,
    belly on the surface,
    accedes to cautious liberation,
    to one stroke of shine-green
    feathers before she darts
    to budding birch.

3. Rickety stairs, uneven surface,
    human scent, do not dissuade
    a naïve bear from
    checking out the deck,
    and so, we meet.
    He reaches the top
    as I venture outside,
    milk-full babe
        ready for a nap *al fresco*
    snuggled in my arms.

    My retreat is slightly faster.

Nechako Flood

That year break-up came too fast:
the ice flowed east in towering chunks
threatened the wooden bridge
jammed at the bend before the confluence
spilled water past the channel
covered farms and yards
across the floodplain
as far as the cut banks.

Consensus ascribed blame to the Creator
for the bitter winter and heavy snow
the warm Spring and early thaw
the way the one river wound and wandered
and rushed before it joined the other,
the beauty of the fertile flat land—
as though God Himself put
those few houses in harm's way.

Singing

2008

Always singing.
Every day, singing.
Grain bucket in hand
        keeps time to her singing.
Newly roused from slumber
garbed in nightclothes
she winds her way to the barn—
        singing.
Back up the hill, empty
pail traces a broader arc—
        singing.

A blessing to take such
joy in this daily chore!

Do I sense no tension,
no caution in her gait?
Why do I suppose joy
brings these songs?

She is singing to the bears.

2018

As dawn's mist ebbs
I make ready to set off.
Struggling with excited dogs
        laden with treats and toys
I walk by that old barn,
cross the woods,
sing to the bears.

Jeanie

Eighteen and ready for adventure
she follows him from Glace Bay to Toronto
serving tables, selling notions,
her pretty face and eastern charm
bagging work to keep them afloat.

When he leaves for the west coast
to finish his degree, she tags along,
really for the roar and tang of the ocean,
and that far-off flat horizon, not for him.

A few years later he drifts east
as she moves north, her BA and
two of his cookie sheets in hand.

One Sassy Crow

I spend my time at the mall
gathering empties the kind folks
with solid houses place beside the bins.
I arrive at sunup and leave late
same as this one sassy crow.

She came for the free lunch
stayed for the glitz,
on a viewpoint at the lake,
spends her time here—
        a short trip as the corvid flies.

After a hearty breakfast at one
fast food joint or the other
she sets up shop—one medium drink
cup angled *just so* beside the curb.

She searches the parking lot for
swag that shines, brings it back
investigates further
evaluates the glitter-factor
looks for bits that wiggle
pries with beak and claw
drops it from a height
        as often as required
to expose the innards.

Slugabed black birds
too lazy to collect their
own booty cruise by.

Before they touch down, she
stashes her treasure in the cup,
hops to the sidewalk,
gazes off as though bored,
waits them out.

Small Bear

This small bear knows what
he knows and he knows *up*.
Planted on the floor he scrambles
up the desk chair, meets at the summit
empty air and the limits of knowledge.

Back on the carpet he tries a different *up*,
scales the bookcase, shudders
as stuff tumbles in his wake,
hunkers on the top.

Passersby found him squalling
under a truck in a parking lot
after dolts chased his mother away—
picked him up and brought him in.

On a bad day, even an average day,
there is no space for an orphan cub.
But today there is an opening,
a bottle, a ride to refuge,
another chance at *up*.

Northern Lights

All the drive home wondering
            Will it last?
this show, these dancers with
flashing eyes and aery robes
this corps of fractured-prism shades
the endless *fouettés en tournant*
across the vast inky stage.

Will it last while we rush
all breathless to the house,
carry drowsy children
wrapped in quilts into
the clear sharp air?

Will it last until we cry,
Look! Look at the streaks,
the colours, the bright arc
above the roof?

Oh, look!

Wild Mint Tea

After the snow melts and water abates
stroll in the back paddock
below the old cottonwoods
foraging for shoots, supple and red.

On a summer day both dry and warm
come back alone
        no nuzzling horse to trample the ground
        or disturb the adept cutting of stalks.
Gather the stems in a cloth bag.
Spread your harvest on a spotless sheet
in a quiet room. Close both
blinds and door with care.

On a brisk Fall day, crush
a few dried leaves,
boil the water, make the tea.

A Girl

The letter regrets to inform
that a girl in Bangladesh
has tumbled from a palm tree.
This child I fed both meat and milk,
sent to school in proper uniform,
        but never met,
has unexpectedly, incredibly, died.

        The old birch below my window
        has three tops, many branches.
        It is lush, verdant, easy to mount.
        The children who climb there
        are safe, are mine still.

Envision her ascent,
her resolve to see the world—
step by measured step,
thick braid swaying,
green ribbon at the end.

I hope her fall was fast or slow,
the ground hard or soft,
her mother near or nearer.

Midwinter Words

Stark words & spare
writ white on white
        chill
        frost
        ice
        snow
                cloud
                wind
                blow
        melt
        flow.

Dull brown above the
white whispers:
green below.

To Look, To See

who would not run
    into
the teeming rain
the gleaming air
the glistening fractured light

into prism-promise

to look beyond
asphalt and cars
school and fence
sodden leaves
hunched backs

to see, stretched across
the luminous vault
Noah's primordial bow

and at the end
where sky meets earth
a token: one sturdy tree
in humble yard
awash with indigo?

Barred Owl

I notice him in fall
patrolling the end field
          sweeping slow
          straight as an arrow
          silent as
                    silent as an owl.
He disappears always in tawny maple
foliage or a thicket of spruce.
I do not see him balance on branch
or swoop to earth.

Today he comes closer.
He rests in a fir tree beyond
the barn—this morning,
in that tall birch below the house.

He cocks his head with mild interest
as I pass in the morning chill.

Has he time on his wings?

Corn in Egypt

She queues at the Liverpool dock
one son, one bag, one ear of bearded wheat
        wrapped in tissue, nestled deep,
two tickets for the *Empress.*

Ahead:
a husband on the CPR, a modest flat,
a strange city in a harsh climate.

Behind:
sisters, servitude, poverty,
the weight of old ways.

A friend gave her the wheat
said there would be corn in Egypt.

Oh, Lord, let there be corn in Egypt.

Before and After

First.
No, not first.
Before.

Air lifts, pivots
dried maple leaves
drooping on the branch.
That modest shift
some scent revived
draws the dog's snout
from the freezing ground,
compels her to enquire of scant cloud,
to evaluate moisture, temperature,
the chance of snow.

Sparse spruce boughs
and naked aspens shiver.
The old dog turns
    (so briefly)
north, sighs deeply,
starts off.

Fine sharp crystals.
After.

The Lamp Post

Descend from sheltered porch to frosted air
pull collar snug against your throat
follow the hoof-marked powder track.

Snow blends with silhouettes—
distant gaping roof and tumbled logs
bare branch bound to bistre trunk
aspen pillars receded to one tenebrous wall.

Brush grand dancing boughs,
release powdery cascades to
tumble off your hood
and kiss your face.

Bend the willow shoots
turn sideways in the eddy
peer into the meadow.

Expect to greet the Lamp Post.

Gleann Eilg: West Beach

So many parts to the whole:
a deep basin, an anchorage
and yet so many parts.

> Generous souls name this narrow stretch
> of weathered stones *the swimming beach*.
> A six-week season for the hardy,
> earliest shiver to last,
> and longer for the dogs.

Start where the main path ends in
blackberry bramble. While the terrier
snuffles in the warren, take a moment
to catch sun-glint on *madrone* bark,
pick your way down boulders to the shore.

Visible parts:
Battered yew log,
loosed from the breakwater,
askew on the beach.
Sea onions, gift of tide and storm.
Otter scat laced with shell.
Gulls and cormorants
preening on the poles.
One sea lion,
upper body of,
afloat.

Hidden parts:
Mollusks, sea stars, jelly fish,
safe in shadow. Osprey in aerie.
The ripples of shoaling herring,
the underwater wake of whale.

Invisible parts:
Birdsong. Salt air.
Rich warm breath.

Gourmet Grilled Cheese

It's a bit of a cheat, selling grilled cheese
sandwiches at the Farmers' Market.
        Grow it, bake it or make it.
I didn't grow it, no real baking and the
making takes five minutes, start to finish.

What's Gourmet Grilled Cheese?
Is it deep fried? It's a sandwich.
The sign doesn't say that.
The sign is incomplete: it's
a grilled cheese sandwich.

I keep a tidy stall—foil to my chaotic life—
ice-cooled ingredients, bleached utensils,
my hair tucked under a paisley scarf.
I wear, of course, a matching apron.

        One sign was reversed in the making,
        reads "Grilled Cheese Gourmet".
        Who is the Grilled Cheese Gourmet?
        You are ... pick your toppings.

The girl with flame bush hair
African basket on her arm
surveys the market offerings;
she always buys a sandwich –
simple food, trusted ingredients.
Mothers pushing laden strollers choose
the white-bread-no-toppings *Classic* to share.
That lovely Swiss baker bought from me once,
after her husband had *eaten her lunch empty.*

All She Desires

I read that a just-birthed babe
laid on the mother's thigh
will hunch, inch, worm and wriggle
to her mother's breast
        given an hour or so.
The notion of a less than helpless infant
attracts, makes some sense, but who
constructs the investigation,
convinces the expectant woman
        to sign on
        then hold back
through sweat and blood
exhaustion and elation
when all she desires
is that fragile form nursing at her side?

To the Shops

I buckle cranky kids
into car seats, close the door
dream of wandering away
        for a minute
when in my mind's eye
beyond the years
down many roads
I observe Margaret Crockett Campbell
        husband's mother's father's mother
leaving her Glasgow flat.

She struggles down steep stone
stairs, bundled bairn in one arm,
wee wagon under t'other,
two young ones close behind.
At roadside she lays Maggie
in the cart, seats James and Jessie
either end, hustles to the shops.
She wants mince from the butcher
tatties from the greengrocer
bread from the baker.
She must hurry back to
make tea for the lot of them—
four boys at school, two at work,
her ailing mother, and dear
Joseph, who is always late.

Her image fades:
I turn back to the car
get in, drive to town.

Night Bus

The night bus traverses terrain
built of moon-shone snow,
crosses towns lit by ground-tied stars—
\ / Edson — Spruce Grove —
Valemount

Children tucked-up in corners
toss about, vexed, amid
rumpled cushions, cozy fleece,
the constant rock and roll,
rattle and sway.

Travelers of small stature
and some experience
stretch along the row—
pillowed heads to window wall
knees curved in, one arm
wedged between the seats.

Others manage as they can
pressed into spots too tight for
comfort, too upright for relax.

Roused by stop and start
on city streets, riders stir
to gather belongings.
They are glad to reach home or
to have left it far behind,
going down the road.

The Moment

Tragedy unfolds when the mother
glances away for the briefest
moment and the child vanishes.
Slid left or right, away from shore,
off the ledge, under a snag,
conscious or unconscious, gone.

Mercy alights when the mother,
in that blessed moment,
does not look away:
the girl grasps at a minnow,
stumbles back once, twice,
tumbles without murmur or splash.

The mother clambers over the bench
all arms and legs, legs and arms
rushes to that site fixed in her gaze.
   One roar:
   the breeze, the chatter,
   the lapping waves.
Her chest tightens with each breath.
She scans the water for ripple, bubble,
foot or hand, loose mantle of hair,
locates the child suspended beneath
the surface—still, eyes staring.

The mother scoops her up
hugs her tight, tighter
awaits indignant wail.

Fearsome Frolic

The newborn hares are
set upon as soon as
they leave the natal hollow.

They scatter in all directions,
follow spokes of an unseen wheel:
The hunter pursues one,
slays it, devours it right there.
That wretched scream stains the air.

The second day repeats
the pattern of the first, except
the wheel is missing one spoke.

With a transient predator
          catching-as-catch-can
this dance of pursuer and pursued
might spare a few leverets.

Here, a seasoned barn cat is in charge:
the fearsome frolic lasts six days.

Winter Score

Freeze-point snow
rides the south wind
icy flakes encase
the copse of firs
bind boughs tight to trunk
create lap over lap
layer upon layer
of scaly crust.

Cue Tchaikovsky's festive score:
enchanted, crystalline columns
shape-shift their rough contours.

Conjure a phalanx:
nutcracker princes on parade
hoary beards, frosted manes
shuffle closer, closer, tap
swords in time against the pane.

Scurry a coterie of angels:
ornate peignoirs trimmed to excess
with alabaster lace and silver wings.

Spin and twirl and pirouette
organza, tulle, silk and satin—
snowflake corps fades
into charcoal night.

Tangerine Tee

Rana Plaza collapse, Dhaka, Bangladesh
24 April 2013

Eva dons a new tangerine Tee
three quarter length sleeve—
        the perfect Wednesday morning
        pick-me-up attire—
spends a moment with her reflection
adds coffee to her mug
runs out the door.

Why the tear, and soot near the hem?
That bit of blood?
Did she snag on the latch?

A swirl of dust, the rising
stench of acrid organic smoke;
the fabric contracts against her ribs.

She brakes suddenly
bolts from the car
struggles from her shirt
hugs her bare chest and gasps for air.
From the open window
she hears the hourly news.

The Pond

I.
There are reasons for this journey:
    puddle-splashing,
    barking and shouting,
    running wild.
The worthy destination? The beaver pond.

Our dog paws at the shallows
spins and wags, whines for a stick.
The boy tosses one and the dog retrieves.
He heaves a rock and the dog swims after.
She edges beside the dam, searches.
Her collar catches; she struggles
churns up muddy water.
I do not jump in because
my son can be trusted—
    oh, he can be trusted—
to follow or run or hide,
but not to stay still.
I dare not move.

The dog emerges, panting,
waterlogged pole in tow.
Undaunted by her adventure,
she drags it behind.

The boy spins an epic yarn.
I dismiss my fear, the false foreboding.
We resolve to come again.

II.

The beavers fail at selective harvest
          craft their own eviction
when they fell trees in the windbreak,
open corridors across the lane.
The landowner reciprocates with
trappers and cages, heavy machines.

We haven't the heart to go back.

Gleann Eilg: New Year's Eve

Forecast: *Rain, at Times Heavy.*
From my vantage: *Heavy Rain.*

Inhabit a Wet Coast winter lexicon:
cheerless, deluge, bucketing, drencher.

Cede to gathering fog, the obscured
far shore and near forest, sealed isolation.

Venture to the barn or roadway
together, or both may be lost.

Light lanterns and candles
for the promise of cheer.

Text your daughter in Moncton
Are you there?

Cargo Flight

Colombia, 1990

The trader stalls before my desk
clutches papers he signed himself
trumpets that insurance cannot cover
what those cows were worth, insists
the innocents suffered at my hand.

The stock suffered this:
one death in exchange
for another, a surprise ending.

Cattle dealer, ask the boy
what he endured,
his third flight above the jungle.
Enquire which memory pains him most:
unbalanced engine sounds
        one steady, one crippled,
the plane's roll as restless creatures shift
        first their hooves
        then their full weight,
        leaning all one way,
or blindfolding them
        binding their legs,
        pushing each beast
        out the cargo door.

Take your money.
Keep your outrage.
We all have jobs to do,
some worse than others.

Killdeer

On our daily warm-up circuit
we spot the killdeer
        posturing
        slanted to one side
        wing dragging
intent on drawing us away.

We dismount at once
lead the horses after the bird
tie them to the fence.
Hands clasped we traverse the ring
west to east, north to south
search the ground for speckled
egg or fledged chick.

The killdeer follows
swings ahead
drops a wing
limps away.

Finding only shavings and dirt,
we take the horses
back the way we came.

Each evening we return on foot
to view the killdeer's dance.
When she doesn't show
we fetch the horses.

The Pearly Gates

Gabriel didn't see the pearly gates:
just his callow grandfather, dead
since his own Maman was six.
He knew the man by stories of
that hooked index finger,
broken as a child.
Grand-père sent him back—
back where he belonged.

White, Gabriel says.
You don't know white.
Blanc, blanc. Pure light.
Splendid shining bright.
Whiter than ghost berry
on the bare branch
against the freshest snow.

He stops stacking wood.
Open hand at chest
rests on old scars.
Silver head lifts,
eyes raise,
contemplating white.

Chance Meeting

Expanse of plate glass between
office wall and floodplain
interrupts hummer-flight
with muted thud.

Rush outside
put him in a box
smear sugar syrup on his beak.
Rufous sides inflate,
deflate, by tiny measure.
Proffer syrup on a spoon.
Tined tongue darts to taste.
Again. And faster.
Eyes open, feet tuck under,
bird rises on wobbly legs.

Run to the lawn
(far from any window)
lift the lid.
Expect … nothing, anything.

Of a sudden he may soar
scribe a ragged vortex
wheel far and high
until sight of him is lost
against cerulean vault.

In the Meadow

Winter chants a single note,
tone poem of one degree:
snow-white   frost-white   ice-white
cold-white   deep-white   dead-white.

The warmth of Spring
coaxes close harmonies
brown of mud of branch and bud
merging shades of green:
    foxtail   timothy   brome
    swamp-grass   cut-grass
yellow-green   blue-green   green-green.

Summer pulls out all the stops
hits every note in a major key
plays it loud and long,
sings colours bold
shouts wildflowers of every hue.

Autumn takes a minor key.
Each supple stem in turn completes
its part, makes an exit in the
symphony of farewells.

Two Snakes

A common garter snake
stretched on the dappled wall
is harmless, nicely posed to lend
his lithe and splendid shape
        scarlet and saffron stripes ashine
to an eponymous entry
in the abecedarium:
he is available, as well,
to decorate for scholars
definitions of sinuous and slither.

        Greet this fellow with subdued smile,
        with nod to happy happenstance.

Weeks later, digging in the pantry
for that last jar of piccalilli,
I detect at the periphery
        tight against the jamb
a gently swaying form,
at least a metre long
thick as my wrist
forked tongue flicking
in and out, side to side.

        Instinct whispers,
        there is no benign snake:
        like Lawrence, I vacillate;
        like Dickinson, I freeze.

The serpent, wisely, does not
budge, reason returns.
I grasp him firmly near the middle
        heedless of unavoidable musk
carry him outside two-handed
set him by the woodpile.

At this latitude, he must be
Snake, Garter, Common.

Another Bird Song

Songbirds return
on wings, on prayers,
on eagle backs
in gusts, in gales
in sheets of rain
in swirls of snow
to frozen ground
to ice on pond
to bare-branch shrub.

They fly alone, in pairs,
in drifting flocks,
with flit and flash.
They peck, they sing,
they build, they stay.

The little birds come home.

Last Words

Bogota, 2000

Probe the book of last words
spoken by the fifty thousand, past
Dear God and *Our Father*
Sweet Jesus, What the Hell and *Oh!*
to these uttered in the back seat
of the sedan: *Es una patata.*

I never liked this road. It skirts
the city slyly, meanders, switches
back, ominous at every curve.
I dislike the unexpected detour,
disconcerting mix of farm trucks and
late commuters, and a motorcycle
that overtakes too close.

It's a bomb!
No, it's a potato.

My leg disintegrates, the upholstery
flies apart, my husband vanishes.
I start to laugh—some potato—
unfasten the seatbelt, close my eyes,
roll out through the flames.

Deliberation at the Green Grocer's

Apples are a good buy considering
drought and deluge
        at the wrong times
        or in the wrong places
and the dollar low
and the times in general.
Six will be enough.
A half dozen oranges, too
        firm, heavy
        priced within means.
I can manage two bags.

He slept not a wink last night
but rose sensible enough to reach
his chair; remembered, even, his glasses
for television and those moments
of rigid sitting, vacant stare.

Twelve pieces of fruit will be fine:
he can hold on that long.

Braggart

A common crow
        fat, glossy, bold
tarries on the power pole below the road
stretches his neck, proclaims his presence
        in brashest voice.
He scribes his way around the top
faces each direction in turn
        cawing, cackling, calling.

He brags of future exploits
warns all comers he is up for action
puts garden birds on notice—
he'll be 'round to check the nests
when their chicks are plump.

To add credence to his bluster
he pitches forward
rockets up
flies a tight circle
flattens wings to body
executes two perfect barrel rolls.

The Sybil of the Rhine

Hildegard von Bingen, 1098-1179

The Abbess
Unlike the sweet girl who tends
my chamber with such concern,
I did not enter with a pure
and open peasant's heart
to become a bride of Christ.

Make no mistake—His mark is on me.
Brought young and ill to the house,
I know the very hand of God and
hear the songs of Heaven peal.
From my pen canticles splash across the page,
and from my throat spill forth, even as I sleep.

I am His visionary; a vessel overflowing.

The Novice
At night I hear such sounds
from the lady's chamber—
strains that leap and soar
voicings of grace
that are not words.

I sweep and scrub
mind her fire, tidy her desk
        linger, linger
to discern how she binds the notes to paper,
weaves harmonies, breathes them life—
holy whispers on the psaltery strings.

The Councillor

Benjamin Gompertz, London 1821

He cuts a fine figure
(thanks in part to his tailor)
and speaks so well:
his manners impeccable,
his connections considerable,
his wife in every way an asset.

Ah, but his mind is brilliant—
he won the Society's contest
so often, they should rename it
for him. The acuity of his theories
upholds the elegance of their themes:
        the aberration of light
        the differential sextant
        the convertible pendulum.

Think where the fellow might
be, had he attended college.
Impossible of course:
        the man is a Jew!

Gleann Eilg: Thistle

Our new place
an old farm
on the brink of ruin,
and of the sea.

Behind the aged barn
a patch of thistle
to warm the Gaelic heart.

The day? Too hot for
cutting thistle, and
too late to be much help.

The unexpected gift:
to comprehend
as soft as thistle-down
by the armload.

Borrowed

One image suggests
and a second confirms
this child of dreams
will not survive outside
haven of the womb.

Minds freeze
guts wrench
hearts bleed.

There are gifts:
the few hushed months
to fashion a gossamer gown,
        a ruffled bonnet, a warm shawl,
to prepare a sacred chamber
        rheostat tuned to their tears
to compose a beginning and an end
each breath upheld by whispered prayer,
no other resting place than a mother's arms.

The possibility after birth
to borrow her
a few minutes longer.

Snow Walking

Confirm:
freeze-thaw cycle
midmorning
brilliant sky
sturdy cleated boots.

Stand:
in the field
in the middle
eyes closed
barefoot.

Feel:
pebbled crust melt
frigid pool
molecules deep
under, around, between.

If my soul was
as clean
as raw
as guileless
as this snow
I might even walk on water.

Homestead

Everyone knew this lake-bottom clay
once cleared of Sub-boreal spruce
was barely fit for hay,
but latecomer Poles
        sharpened by lean times
        ocean sickness
        tedious grimy trains
coveted the southwest aspect
for a house, frost-sheltered patch
below the bank for garden.
They snared hare for hearty stew,
built a pale and wire fence
to keep cow in and coyotes out.

Those immigrants long dead,
the grandchildren do not farm.
But, pasture turned meadow,
that bent lilac bush,
the broken cabin
        roof beams tumbled to stone hearth
remember.

Victorian Christmas

Seeking diversion from the rain,
we visit the Victorian Hall.
Inside, the house is cool,
the decor dim and dismal.
The mean fire in the grate
cannot make amends.
The children fuss.

Off to the museum next door, to tour
relics in a brighter, warmer setting.
Our son is content among wringer washers,
butter churns, mechanical toys with cranks.

But our daughter of tender heart stops
stock still, pale as pale, eyes wide.
She has discovered sparrows behind glass.

They are dead.
Yes, I agree. They are dead.
Someone killed them; they are dead.
I concur: they are dead.

The Victorians were so strange:
bugs on pins, stuffed kittens in clothes,
birds mounted for display.
I want to explain, to say—
But. It wasn't me. It wasn't us.

She is just three and cares
nothing about old customs;
she cares about wrongs
done and these lifeless birds.
As she spins on her heels
and turns away, she
repeats one last time,
They are dead.

Yes, I agree. They are dead. I am so sorry.

Mercy and Grace

They hang at the window
gather on the threshold
these fragments
these few words.

They fall from my pen
as songs of mercy and grace
of soft-breathed thanks.

Lifeline

Each prairie farm holds the tale—
somebody saved by the rope
anchoring house to barn,
or legend of the scofflaw
neighbour lost, not found 'til Spring,
too self-assured to fix a loosened end.
        Stretched across utter white, that line is life.

On this plateau of textured terrain
of graded slopes and brush
we carry on without a rope.
When, baffled by winter storm,
sleep delayed or moonless night,
I happen upon the fence,
the brain-map etched by scores
of trips brings me home.

Clambering from the drift,
wet and cold, short one boot,
        I ache for a sure connection.

Two Doors

She paints the door red—
        not the front entry off the drive—
the side door that opens onto
stone terrace and rocky path
that skirts the down-sloped yard.

He coats broad sliding panels
at the barn with oxblood stain
        turns weathered surface carmine
installs bulbs in old fixtures
mounted on the near gable wall.

She sets a loaf of bread on the table.

He walks east from the yard
when beasts are bedded
the old tractor parked
and summer sun sets,
gazes homeward
to a slash of crimson.

She glances out a high window,
detects outbuildings blending
with ground in the gloaming.
As the light fades, she catches
sight of his tinted door.

Leaving

We all left the island
answered our mother's prayers:
six women living in Toronto
savouring island food
relishing island time
once a year, at Caribana.

Some slaved as domestics
got through teacher's college.
I attended nursing school—free—
worked fingers to the bone
persevered without sleep.

Mother would not leave:
stayed to the end in a place
where a three-year-old told her
You must call me Master Henry:
she replied *Not while I wipe your bum!*
walked out the door, quit
that house for the last time.

Died of Wounds

William Thomas Hurst, 1918

Our Billy:
gently bathed, free at last
of damp and slime,
laid out among the fallen—
those with limbs lost,
holes right through,
perished while
drugged, awake, asleep,
sensible or fever-wracked.
They died of wounds.

Want, excess,
virus, sepsis,
epidemic, endemic,
chronic, acute,
annihilated, surrendered:
flat-lined and lain
on a narrow bed.

Mark this: We all die of wounds.

De Trop

Hard packed drifts force the ermine
from cover, toward the backroad
in search of secluded lairs.

Greasy scent of stout domestic fowl
pervades the night, engulfs her,
draws her from the woods.
        A sliver of silver moonlight
        crosses open ground,
        slides up the post,
        steals into the pen.

The ravaged flock shapes
a tidy row of surplus kill.
She struggles with each mort in turn—
cannot comprehend this shelter
where creatures enter but may not leave.
        After a meagre meal she
        carries away a mouthful.

Grocery Shopping

Some country folk
    unfamiliar with the winged
    clients at this mall
have gone for coffee,
plastic bags of groceries lying
in the box of their old truck.

The local committee of crows soon
assembles on the pickup's cab.
Each selects a bag and gets busy:
    spread the handles
    sort the contents—
    no tears, no beak marks
    no excrement.

A quick confab confirms the menu:
the leader lifts off awkwardly
trailing a string of sausages.
His confederates fall in behind,
like a parade of gluttonous
mourners making for a wake.

Vernal Equinox

There is here no sharp divide:
Spring-start, Winter-end.
Like right and left hands
in Rachmaninoff's prelude,
the seasons chase back and forth
one on top, one below
always in danger
of locking thumbs.

Did it rain before last snow
or thaw before the freeze?

March equinox trades
an hour of night for day,
proffers a reminder
to advance timer
on the grow-light
a hair's breadth.

Mrs. Woodcock's Garden

We had the run of Mrs. Woodcock's yard
        (in a way/almost)
feet glued to concrete track.
The walkway from the city street
dissected the front lawn neatly
conformed to other sidewalks
on that tidy avenue.

A lesser path hugged the house
wrapped the mossy corner
halted at the cedar gate where
        fastened to the latch
trailed a rope for our hands.

The first rule kept us
on the narrow way,
the second closed that gate
after we slid through.
Fair price to pay for entry
to garden grown wild with
berries and unkempt bushes,
ruled by mammoth cats,
each too staid to hop a fence.

We did not eat the fruit
or steal the flowers.
We did not free the cats.
We were not too young
to understand, perfectly,
the tenets of a bargain.

This Orange

I choose this orange for the heft
that promises thin skin, dense fruit,
and for its pleasant ovoid form.

The distance covered triggers
no carbon footprint alarms—
free sunshine in season, slow boat,
cardboard crate all considered.

> There is the matter of illegal aliens
> inhabiting a horse stable in Mpumalanga,
> but conditions really aren't bad;
> there is work, there is food on the table.
> *Hush. Enough said. Aren't I well-situated*
> *on someone's ancient land?*

I peel the fruit, remove rind and central column,
separate the segments, slice each precisely in half.
Anticipation greets disappointment with
the first bite: too much fibre, too little juice.

Stoically, I consume the whole,
fletcherise each morsel.

This orange grew so large, came so far,
adorned the pottery bowl so well:
what else was I to do?

Questions for the Man Who Would Mind My Cat

Embedded quote from "Anthem" by
consummate artist, Leonard Cohen

How do you feel about enjambment-interrupted:
The first line employs no punctuation
But the next starts with an uppercase letter
That stops you in your tracks?

What about
enjambment-exceeded
line after
line rambling on and
on to some tired and
tiresome, longed for
conclusion and best
of all, an end-stop. Period.
And question mark.

What would you throw into
that stinking kettle of fish?
Unnecessary rhyme?
Forced rhyme?
Rhyme without rhythm
or at its expense?

Consider the laziness of the false rhyme,
a single word repeated three
times, passed off as rhyme.

What do you make of this?
Ah, the wars
They will be fought again
The holy dove
She will be caught again
Bought and sold
And bought again…

Acknowledgements

I am enormously grateful to longtime friend and sympathetic critic, P.N. van den Bosch, for his insight, his encouragement, and his knowledge of and delight in language and literature.

Publication Notes

Earlier versions of some poems in this collection have been published previously:
"Three Black Dogs", *The Nashwaak Review*, Summer/Fall 2012, vol. 28/29, no. 1.
"Lifeline", © *Christian Century*, 10 July 2013, vol. 130, no. 14.
"Swimmers", "Jeanie", *The Nashwaak Review*, Summer/Fall 2013 vol. 30/31, no. 1.
"Braggart", *Passion: Poetry*, vol. 1, no. 1.
"Thresholds", *Literary Review of Canada*, vol. 21, no. 8.
"Winter Lexicon", *Arc Poetry Magazine*, Fall 2013.
"At Ten to Eight", *Forgetting Home: Poems about Alzheimer's*, Anna Evans, editor.
"Night Bus", *The Prairie Journal*, no. 61.
"Homestead", *Queen's Quarterly*, vol. 121, no. 2.
"Two Snakes", *The Nashwaak Review*, Summer/Fall 2014 vol. 32/33, no. 1.
"Late November, -10C", *Freefall*, vol. 26, no. 1.
"Deliberations at the Green Grocer's", "The Flood", "This Orange", "The Sybil of the Rhine", *The Nashwaak Review*, Summer/Fall 2016 vol. 36/37, no. 1.
"Last Words", *geez*, no. 48.
"De Trops", "Two Doors", "Questions for the Man Who Would Mind My Cat", "Gleann Eilg: Thistles", *The Nashwaak Review*, Summer/Fall 2017, vol. 38/39, no. 1.
"Wild Mint Tea", *Queen's Quarterly*, vol. 125, no. 2.
"Barred Owl", "Died of Wounds", "Lights", "Little Junco", "Singing", *The Nashwaak Review*, Fall/Winter 2018/2019, vol. 40/41, no. 1.
"A Girl", *geez*, no. 53.

"Small Bear", "The Pond", *The Nashwaak Review*, Fall/Winter 2019/2020, vol. 42/43, no. 1.
"Corn in Egypt", "Leaving", *Feminist Gift Economy: A Maternalist Alternative to Patriarchy and Capitalism, Canadian Woman Studies/les cahiers de la femme 34.1,2* (Fall/Winter 2019).
"Ever-After Birds", *The Antigonish Review*, Volume 50, Number 203, Fall 2020.